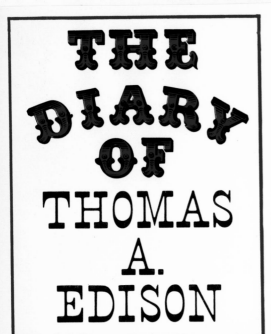

THE DIARY OF THOMAS A. EDISON

Introduction by
KATHLEEN L. McGUIRK

Thomas Edison's famous 1885 *Diary,* reproduced in facsimile, reflects a facet of the inventor's genius which is seldom found in his volumes of scientific papers and letters. Here, writing in a rare spirit of relaxation and amusement, Edison allows his intimate thoughts to flow freely. His puckish humor and keen sense of human foibles focus on the Victorian world around him during a short period of his life occupied solely by frivolous activities on the Massachusetts shore.

Edison's perceptive observations cover a multitude of subjects, including thoughts on contemporary literature, an hilarious account of an empty-headed drugstore clerk, a performance by Lillian Russell in a stifling Boston theater, the abuse of tobacco, trends in fashion and the shortcomings of political figures. Throughout the *Diary* he talks of picnics and boat rides with "Mama G." and Ezra Gilliland, with whom he was staying, and Daisy Gaston, another guest. Above all, his mind returns daily to his love for Mina Miller, who would soon become his second wife.

Edison kept this *Diary* as an exercise in parlor wit, intending it to be read aloud for the amusement of his friends and never dreaming it would someday be published. Yet, with the light touch of the poet, he proves his ability to excel in literary invention. His precise handwriting, occasional misspellings and afterthought editing combine with an astonishing breadth of non-scientific observations to give a remarkable insight into the personality of one of America's most brilliant minds.

KATHLEEN L. McGUIRK, Archivist at the Edison National Historic Site in West Orange, New Jersey, has worked for nearly twenty years with the vast collection of Edison papers assembled at West Orange, and is perhaps more familiar than anyone with his public and personal life. In her Introduction, Mrs. McGuirk presents a capsule biography of Edison's life, with emphasis on the period during which he wrote the *Diary.* Over thirty photographs (some previously unpublished), drawings and documents show Edison, his family, individuals mentioned in the *Diary,* and Winthrop, Massachusetts, where the *Diary* was written, as it looked around 1885.

THE
DIARY
OF
THOMAS
A.
EDISON

ETCHED BY
EVANS 1914

KELLY

Thomas A. Edison

January 15 1882.

FROM SITTING AT
104 GOERICK ST

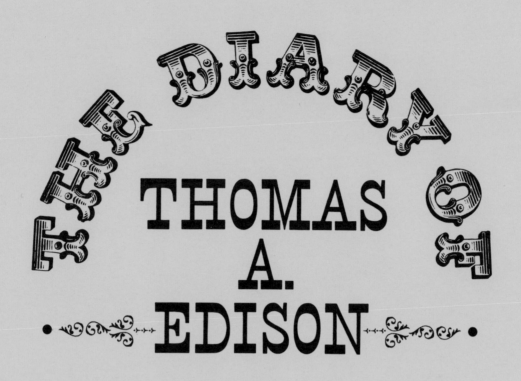

THE DIARY OF THOMAS A. EDISON

Introduction by
KATHLEEN L. McGUIRK

THE CHATHAM PRESS, INC.
Old Greenwich, Connecticut

Distributed by The Viking Press, Inc.

ILLUSTRATION CREDITS: Edison family photographs are courtesy of Edison National Historic Site unless otherwise specified. Early drawings and photographs of Winthrop, Mass. are courtesy of Andrew P. Quigley. Photograph of Woodside Park, 1970 by John V. Hinshaw.

This book is produced in cooperation with the United States Department of the Interior, National Park Service, Edison National Historic Site, West Orange, New Jersey. The original manuscript of The Diary of Thomas A. Edison and the Introduction to the facsimile publication prepared by Kathleen L. McGuirk are in United States Government ownership at the Edison National Historic Site. As such they are in public domain. Copyright on this book is limited to prohibition against direct copying from the pages thereof without written consent from the Chatham Press, Inc., Old Greenwich, Connecticut.

SBN 85699-017-5 (Clothbound edition)
SBN 85699-018-3 (Paperbound edition)

Library of Congress Catalog Card Number: 71-107081

Manufactured in the United States of America
by The Eastern Press, Inc., New Haven, Connecticut

CONTENTS

Thomas Edison at the age of 14.

Samuel Edison, Thomas Edison's father.

Edison's electrical vote recorder.

INTRODUCTION

THE Diary of Thomas A. Edison, reproduced in full in this book, is the only diary Edison ever kept. Written in July, 1885, during his first sustained respite from work in almost twenty-six years, this remarkable document gives a rare insight into the lighter side of Edison's character. It represents an emergence from the disruption of his personal life caused by the death of his first wife, Mary, in August 1884, and the awakening of new confidence which led to his remarriage. In this sense it marks an important milestone in Edison's personal life, as well as the beginning of the second phase of his career in a new home and laboratory at West Orange, New Jersey.

Thomas Alva Edison's scientific career began in 1859 when, at the age of twelve, he gained reluctant permission from his parents to take a job as a newsboy and "candy butcher" on the Grand Trunk Railway which ran between Port Huron, Michigan and Detroit. A tolerant guard allowed him to set up a small laboratory in the baggage car where he spent every spare moment experimenting. From then on, with the exception of the period shortly before and after this Diary was written, his single-minded dedication to science and invention never ceased.

At sixteen Edison became a telegraph operator for the Western Union Telegraph Company. His beautifully clear handwriting, in which he was to pen the Diary many years later, was his own style, cultivated for legibility and speed during long nights transcribing Morse code. The few grammatical errors found in the Diary rarely appear in his technical writings and, one suspects, were a deliberate attempt to appear unpretentious.

Edison's first patent, granted in October 1868, was for an electrical vote recorder. It worked only too well! One of the greatest weapons in the hands of a minority party was filibustering and Edison's machine, which greatly speeded up the tally of votes, was most unwelcome. From then on he concentrated on inventing things that were not only useful, but in greater demand.

He turned his attention to the telegraph. His many improvements in telegraphic printers and stock tickers earned him the money to start his own manufacturing business

"The Wizard of Menlo Park" in 1880.

Edison's laboratory at Menlo Park. (This building has been fully restored and now stands in Greenfield Village, Dearborn, Michigan.)

in Newark, New Jersey. By 1871, he was able to tell his parents in Port Huron: "I have a large amount of business to attend to. I have one shop which employs 18 men and am fitting up another which will employ 150 men." He added, with wry, self-deprecating humor, "I am now what you democrats call a 'Bloated Eastern Manufacturer'."

On Christmas Day of that year Edison married Mary Stilwell, a shy, young girl who had been working in his Newark shop. Five years later, in 1876, he moved into his famous laboratory at Menlo Park. During the following six years his fame spread widely and he became known as "The Wizard of Menlo Park."

In 1882, having outgrown this laboratory and needing to be nearer the center of commerce, he began to move his base of operations to New York City. The phonograph, while causing a great sensation at the time of its invention in late 1877, had taken a back seat for the more complicated task of devising and inventing, step by step, a complete central station electric lighting system. To provide the hundreds of parts needed for this enterprise, Edison established manufacturing plants in Harrison, New Jersey, and New York City.

Edison now had three children. Marion, or "Dot" as he had nicknamed her, was nine years old; Thomas Jr., affectionately called "Dash," was six; and the baby, William Leslie, was four. The family occupied a pleasant house at 25 Gramercy Park, New York City, and spent summers at Menlo Park, with an occasional trip to Florida.

Mary Stilwell Edison, about 1881.

Marion Edison; 1883.

William Leslie and Thomas Edison, Jr.; 1883.

The Edison home in Menlo Park; 1881.

Then, on August 9, 1884, came the crushing blow. Mary Edison died of typhoid fever at their Menlo Park home after a brief illness. The morning after her mother's death, young Marion found her father so shaken with grief that "he could hardly tell me that mother had died in the night."

Shortly after Mary's death, Edison went to Philadelphia to supervise an exhibition of his electrical inventions being held at the Franklin Institute. His two young sons were left in the care of their maternal grandmother, Mrs. Margaret Stilwell, while Marion, who had hardly left her father's side since her mother's death, accompanied him.

At the Philadelphia exhibition Edison encountered Ezra Torrance Gilliland, a handsome, jovial friend from his telegraph days. Born the same year as Edison, Gilliland was considered an expert in the telephone field and had designed a telephone exchange system for the Bell Company. Nicknamed "Damon and Pythias" in their earlier days, Edison used the name "Damon" for Ezra Gilliland when referring to him in the Diary. The two old friends found much to talk about for Edison's telephone patents had been acquired by the Bell Company, which had also retained his services as a consultant.

Ezra Gilliland was married to the former Miss Lillian Johnson of Indianapolis, a young, attractive and sociable lady referred to affectionately in the Diary as "Mamma G." She was, apparently, a born matchmaker and was destined to have a profound influence on the life of the inventor by introducing him to his future wife. Toward the end of February, 1885, tired and worn after a severe winter illness, Edison made a trip to Florida with Marion and the Gillilands. Upon their return he once more was able to throw himself into his work with vigor, hiring more people, and working nights.

His renewed association with Gilliland and his attractive wife, followed by a visit to their hospitable home while on a business trip to Boston, made Edison keenly aware of his own unsettled and lonely state. Many years later his daughter was to recall: "Soon Father came to the conclusion that he wanted a home, a wife, and a mother for his three children, and he asked Mrs. Gilliland, who lived in Boston, to introduce him to a suitable girl. . . ."

Mrs. Gilliland had a friend from Indianapolis, Miss Louise Igoe, who was living or visiting in Boston that spring. Miss Igoe in turn had a close friend, Jane Miller of Akron, Ohio, whose younger sister, Mina, was studying music at a school in Boston. Louise introduced Mina to the Gillilands, who eventually invited her to a dinner party where she first met Thomas Edison. Mina, who was asked to give a recital for the group, recollected many years later: "I never played for anybody, but they asked me to play, so I thought 'Oh well, I'll never see these people again,' so I played." Regarding Mr. Edison she was asked: "How did he strike you at the time?" and she answered: "Just a genial, lovely man."

Ezra T. Gilliland; date unknown.

Mina Miller; about 1885.

Edison, however, was completely conquered. From then through the rest of that summer he was rarely in New York. His assistants kept him apprised of business matters by mail and telegram, interspersed with the frequent question "when will you return?" His secretary, Samuel Insull, valiantly handled proposals of marriage and applications for the position of governess to Edison's three children. Edison, while keeping a remote finger on the pulse of his world-wide enterprises, seemed a completely changed person. The man who since childhood had been constantly pressed for time, begrudging even the hours spent in sleeping and eating, was suddenly becoming a social figure.

The Gillilands had rented one of six beach cottages in a secluded area of Winthrop known as Woodside Park, not far from the famous Cottage Park resort. Winthrop, located on the north side of Boston Harbor, was considered at the time to be "about the only desirable seaside town within easy reach of Boston for summer and permanent residence" according to the promoters of the Cottage Park Hotel. Trains to Boston ran every fifteen minutes during the summer and every half hour in winter; steamships ferried passengers hourly to the Atlantic Avenue dock with stops at Cottage Park in summer. It was a place to which the wealthier residents of Boston could retreat for the summer to enjoy swimming, sailing and socializing in the cool ocean breezes.

Toward the end of June the Gillilands invited Edison to join them at Woodside Park. The local *Beachmont and Winthrop Visitor* noted his arrival in their issue of Friday, June 25th, 1885: "Mr. Thomas A. Edison, the inventor, of New York, and Miss Daisy Gaston of Indianapolis, are visiting Mr. and Mrs. Gillilands (sic.) at Woodside Park for a few days. There will be a very lively time at Woodside Park July 4th. The committee of arrangements have a great treat in store to celebrate that glorious day." Edison, undoubtedly aware of the "great treat," scribbled a hurried note to Insull which ended: "Could you come over here to spend 4th at Gills . . . There is lots pretty girls . . ."

During the hot summer hours much of one's time was spent in playing various parlor games such as "memory-scheme" and "'pon honor" which Edison describes on page 30 of the Diary, or in reading aloud to each other from books or one's own composition. This Diary, written mostly (or perhaps entirely) at the Gilliland's "Woodside Villa," was kept in a spirit of fun at the only time in his life when Edison indulged himself in such fashionable idling. Alien as the occupation was for him, the keen insight and wit which he displayed demonstrated that when he put his mind to creative writing, he excelled in that as much as in everything else he approached.

Winthrop Center Railroad Station in the late 1800's.

Woodside Park; July 1970.

Throughout the Diary Edison's mind returns to thoughts of Mina Miller. ". . . got thinking about Mina and came near being run over by a street car," he wrote, "If Mina interferes much more will have to take out an accident policy." While the Gillilands also invited many other young ladies to meet their friend, it was clear even to twelve-year-old Marion that, although she had selected Louise Igoe as her choice for a stepmother, her father was "in love with the Ohio girl, Mina Miller."

Mina's father, Lewis Miller, was the inventor of the Buckeye Reaper, as well as co-founder with Bishop John Vincent of the Chautauqua Association in Chautauqua, New York. Miller's strong, independent character, religious beliefs and devotion to scholarship led Edison to remark in later years: "Mr. Miller is better versed in more subjects than any man I know." The family residence, known as "Oak Place," was a large, elegant, though comfortable home in Akron, Ohio. While her father was strict and did not, for example, allow his children to indulge in dancing, Mina's social life was not unduly restricted and she undoubtedly had many suitors. A newspaper article of 1886 described her as ". . . the sweetest girl in the State of Ohio . . . a brunette, with classic features, rich black hair and great dazzling eyes."

THE

Beachmont & Winthrop

VISITOR,

—AND—

REVERE BEACH CHRONICLE.

PUBLISHED EVERY FRIDAY AFTERNOON

SUBSCRIPTION, FOR THE YEAR, $1.50; SIX
MONTHS, $1 (In advance); SINGLE
COPIES, 5 CTS.

All communications should be addressed
to the Publishers, J. H. HARTLEY & Co., 71
Oliver St., Boston, Mass.

The following graduated from the high school yesterday: Miss Lillian B. Belcher, Miss Agnes E. Phillips, Miss Sarah W. Pierce, Clarence L. Bemis and Thomas S. Floyd.

Mr. Thomas A. Edison, the inventor, of New York, and Miss Daisy Gaston of Indianapolis, are visiting Mr. and Mrs. Gillilands at Woodside Park for a few days.

There will be a very lively time at Woodside Park July 4th. The committee of arrangements have a great treat in store to celebrate that glorious day.

Miss Jennie Bird and Miss Ida Floyd conceived the idea of presenting their teacher with some slight token of esteem in which she was held by her scholars of the grammar school last week and took up a

Cottage Park Hotel in Winthrop in the late 1800's.
On the right is one of the Boston ferry boat landings.

During the months after meeting Mina, whom he fondly called his "Maid of Chautauqua," Edison probably bought more clothes than he had in all his previous life. He purchased expensive suits, overcoats, trousers, custom-made shirts by the dozen and, as he writes on page 39 of the Diary, "For the first time in my life I have bought a pair of premeditatedly tight shoes...." His reading habits changed also. Instead of acquiring books of a strictly scientific nature as was his custom, he now purchased such titles as *Insectivorous Plants,* Well's *Physiognomy, Self Help, Character and People,* and others mentioned in the Diary which gave him a reserve of sophisticated small talk required by the elegant world to which Mina belonged. Insull, to whom bills for items such as these were sent for payment, was probably more puzzled than exasperated when he wrote

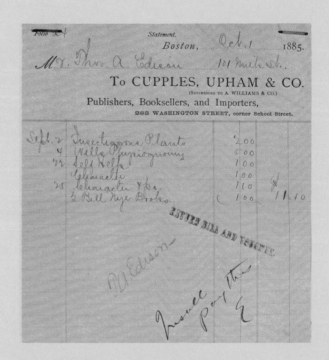

Edison at the end of a long report: ". . . please try to give sufficient time away from plea-sure to write me full instructions . . . and if your inclination requires a little spurring up remember that we have a large amount of money at stake in the matter."

The August 7th issue of the *Visitor* announced: "Mr. Thomas A. Edison and daugh-ter left Woodside Park Tuesday evening for New York to view the funeral procession of the late Gen. Grant from Mr. Edison's private residence, after which they go to Niagara Falls, Thousand Islands, etc. They will return in about ten days." On their way to Niagara Falls, however, Edison and Marion stopped at Chautauqua for a few day's visit with members of the Miller family and ministers from all over the country who had gathered there. Edison, as he himself said, was "not much for religion," but thought it necessary to become better acquainted with the family of the girl he planned to make his bride. Mina and Edison were the subject of much interest as they rode on a crowded ex-cursion steamer around Lake Chautauqua. Edison also planned to take a trip to the White Mountains of New Hampshire with Marion and the Gillilands, and asked his fu-ture father-in-law if Mina could be one of the group. Mr. Miller, at first reluctant, finally gave his consent.

The party set off on August 28. During this trip Marion recalled seeing her father "tap in Morse Code a proposal of marriage on the hand of Miss Miller, for she blushed and nodded yes." Edison later testified: "I taught the lady of my heart the Morse Code, and when she could send and receive we got along much better than we could have with

spoken words by tapping our remarks to one another on our hands. Presently I asked her thus in Morse Code, if she would marry me. The word 'Yes' is an easy one to send by telegraphic signals, and she sent it. . . . Nobody knew anything about many of our conversations on a long drive in the White Mountains, we could use pet names without the least embarrassment, although there were three other people in the carriage." Edison did not expect to be observed by his keen-eyed daughter, who in her own words "rarely missed a trick!"

Upon returning to New York, Edison composed and sent a formal application to Mina's father asking for her hand in marriage. Mr. and Mrs. Miller approved the match, and plans moved ahead for a February wedding. Stories appeared in the newspapers, and as one writer put it, "The luck of that man Edison does beat the record!"

Late in December, Edison showed his bride-to-be a home he had been offered in Llewellyn Park, an attractive private residential section of West Orange, New Jersey. He gave Mina her choice of living in the city or the country, and she chose the country. It was a beautiful home with a great number of expensive furnishings as well as a fine library. The estate was aptly named "Glenmont," for it had been built on a high ridge above a charming glen. It had numerous outbuildings and greenhouses, lawns, and gracefully landscaped gardens.

ABOVE: The library at Glenmont.

LEFT: Glenmont in the 1890's.

natural humor, was notable for
ment, and discrimination. While
...ing with the farcical spirit of the
..ss Rehan's acting was invariably
aggeration, and the most improb-
. derived from her perfect sin-
.naturalness the semblance of
..re is small opportunity in
. Miss Rehan to display her
.otress of high comedy; but
..t II., and a passage in the last
. scheme having succeeded, Nancy,
..eing jubilant, is overcome by
. or the vexations she has
. actress gave glimpses of
.lishments in that direction.
.Mr. John Drew made plain the
..riving due force to broadly comic
.t omitting elegance and grace in
.iction. Mr. Lewis in Griffing has
.is favorite parts. He was quaint
in everything, his wig was
.and where he bought his
.mystery. Mrs. Gilbert, Misses
.ingdon, Messrs. Skinner, Gilbert,
.od made much of sketchy charac-
..rwin contributed another comic
..rkward Irish girl, and Mr. George
.well young man with an idiotic
.ondness for using the diminutive
.on. "Nancy and Company" while
.l afford capital amusement. As
.another new play in rehearsal its
.not likely to be very long. The
.'s Theatre will end on the 1st of

.-AVENUE THEATRE.

. Cibber adaptation of "Rich-
.presented to a large audience at
.nue Theatre last evening by Mr.
.and the Boston Museum company.
. portrayal of the ambitious and
.r who paved the way to the Eng-
..th murderous crime is familiar to
.oers. By bringing out most prom-
.nental shrewdness and physical
.the misshapen and ill-begotten
. Booth is enabled to make the
.ng. From the nature of things,
. impossible to render the char-
..ve or calculated to appeal to
.be singular wooing of the wid-
..Anne, the dissembling at the
..rd Mayor and populace, and the
.final appeal to arms were all given
.rhness that was most praiseworthy.
. greeted with much applause, and
.nes recalled before the curtain.
.y Russell, as the little Duke of
.uished himself in a fine juvenile
. Mr. J. B. Mason, who personated
.ichmond, was fair. This evening
." will be repeated. To-morrow and
.lius Cæsar" will be the play.

.OLITAN OPERA HOUSE.

. evening representation of
.f Sheba" drew an audience of the
.ions to the Metropolitan Opera
..ning. Goldmark's melodious and
.ins have worn better than was
..ticipated. The superb scenic
. which the work is equipped
..se, been an important factor
.but something more than brilliant
.e stage costume is needed nowa-
.an opera with durable attractive-
.not be conceded that the score of

.aitton's music is largely represented among
the glees chosen for performance.

The concert in aid of the Bayreuth fund
occurs at the Metropolitan Opera House this
evening. With the exception of the "Eroica"
symphony and the "Leonore" overture, No. 3,
the programme is made up of excerpts from
Wagner's works.

MR. EDISON'S WEDDING.

THE ELECTRICIAN MARRIED TO A MILLION-
AIRE'S DAUGHTER.

AKRON, Ohio, Feb. 24.—Thomas A. Edison and Miss Mira, daughter of Lewis Miller, of
this city, President of the Chautauqua Assem-
bly and millionaire manufacturer, were married
at 3 P. M. to-day. The nuptials were solemn-
ized at the Miller mansion at Oak Place,
a picturesque spot in the western part
of the city, looking down on Akron's busy
streets. Upward of 100 guests, abut equally di-
vided between Akron and points abroad, and
including only relatives and near friends
of the contracting parties, were in attendance. A beautiful altar, covered with
white, and the white in turn almost
hidden under calla lilies and Maréchal Niel and
tea roses, had been erected in the parlor, and
before it the bride and groom kneeled as they
received the benediction of the officiating cler-
gyman, the Rev. K. Young, D. D., Pastor
of the First Methodist Episcopal Church of
this city. The marriage service of the
Methodist Episcopal Church was employed.
The groom's best man was Lieut. F. W. Tappan,
of New-York. The bride was given away by her
father. There were no bridesmaids. The
bridal costume was of white silk, trimmed
with Duchesse and point lace, square neck,
laced corsage, plain trim. She wore
as ornaments a diamond and pearl
necklace, the gift of the groom. Mr. Edison was
attired in a black Prince Albert, black tie, and
his hands were ungloved.

Congratulations were received under an im-
mense floral wish bone, composed princi-
pally of roses. The other floral pieces
were equally elaborate. New-York and
Cleveland florists were lavishly drawn
upon. The presents made up a rich and costly
array, including every article known to the sil-
ver worker's art, diamond bracelets, diamonds,
ruby and sapphire pin, a column of onyx with
gold capital, and a host of rare articles of
virtu. Dinner was served to the guests, all
comfortably seated at the table at once, and
was supervised by a chef from Chicago, who
brought along a corps of 15 waiters. Among
scores of telegrams of congratulation was one
from Mr. Edison's employes in New-York.
From Gotham there came by special train the
following gentlemen associated with Mr. Edison:
Edward N. Johnson, Charles Batchelor, John
Tomlinson, Samuel Insall, G. Sims, S. Bergmann,
and Charles Bruch. Mr. and Mrs. Edison left on
the 7 o'clock train for Cincinnati, and proceed
directly to their Winter home in Fort Myers
Fla.

MARY AT HOME.

From the Augusta (Ga.) Chronicle, Feb. 23.

Ten years ago a bright and ambitious
country girl, filled with the fire of the stage and
stamped by the hoyden of Kentucky, strode
from the flies in heroine drama. At that time

I have so much that needs attention
need a secretary, which I can't ver.
here, and much of it must be given
attention. So I'm going over to ge.
to get away from the pressure that
be resisted here, and to attend to
affairs. I have engaged passage fo.
but I shall not remain away very
I go I shall remain out here, with
weekly trip to Boston, and I do.
make any appearance in public ag.
go, if I can possibly escape it. You.
how I dislike that sort of thing. P.
ing is positively the most distast.
have to meet. I had to say some.
frequently when I was away, b.
imagine how I disliked it, and I'm.
cane it if it is a possible thing to .
quiet simplicity of Deerfoot is ev.
more congenial to me, and my inc.
lead me to just such a delightful life
lead out here in the very midst of n.
You may say that I don't feel at all
pect to celebrate Washington's bir.
times yet. Good day."

GROVER NOT A SAIN.

From the Detroit Tribune, Fe.

Mr. Carl Dettloff, the German.
father of a round dozen of boys, and.
ious that President Cleveland shoul.
sor for the last addition to his famil.
received the following letter from.
dent:

EXECUTIVE M.
WASHINGTON, Fe.

Carl Dettloff, Esq.:
MY DEAR SIR: I have received you.
tion, in which you are joined by your w.
me of the birth of your twelfth son and.
nation to bestow upon him my name.
the assurance of my appreciation of the.
which induces you to thus make my na.
one in your household, while I express n.
ingness to be represented as sponsor at.
ceremony of your son, which will give to.
Yours, very truly, GROVER CL.

Mr. Dettloff is not entirely satisf.
response. The President cannot.
father to the child unless he is pers.
ent at its baptism, and there is .
whether any priest of the Catholic.
be found willing to bestow the nam.
Cleveland upon the infant. The Re.
once refused to christen a chil.
Cleveland" upon the ground that t.
law required that the name of a sai.
the child. Mr. Dettloff will write .
President, and, if the latter cannot r.
venient to visit Detroit, the child w.
to Washington and christened in th.
vided Mr. Cleveland will promise t.
church and stand sponsor.

PENSIONS TRANSFERRED TO E.

Washington Dispatch to the St. Louis .

Within a short time past seve.
soldiers who are on the pension ro.
liberately arranged to transfer the.
receive to indigent and disabled sur.
lost cause. Gen. Stith Bolling, of.
Va., a prominent ex-Confederate .
the following history of the matt.
time in December last it came to m.
that a gallant and patriotic ex-U.
living at Watertown, N. Y., desir.
pension which had just been a.
should be bestowed upon son.
federate whose wounds made it .
for him to undergo the har.
labor of a well man. I sugge.

From the *New York Times,* Thursday, February 25, 1886.

A bachelor dinner was given for Edison by a few close friends at Delmonico's in New York on February 20, 1886. The wedding, which took place on February 24 at Oak Place, was the event of the year. Mina, wearing white silk duchesse point lace, was radiant. Their honeymoon was spent in Florida, and on their return they set up housekeeping at Glenmont. Mina Miller Edison, at the age of twenty, became the gracious chatelaine of a substantial estate, managing ten servants and caring for three children and a husband; a heavy burden for one so young. She proved herself equal to the task, fulfilling her job splendidly with the full awareness that her husband was one of the most noted and sought-after men of his time. Three children, Madeleine, Charles and Theodore, were born to Thomas and Mina at Glenmont.

In West Orange, a short distance from his home, Edison planned and built a new laboratory to which he and his assistants moved on Thanksgiving Day, 1887. He supervised its construction himself, describing the structure in one of his laboratory notebooks: "My laboratory will soon be completed — The dimensions are one building 250 ft long 50 wide & 3 stories 4 other bldgs 25 x 100 one story high all of brick I will have the best equipped & largest Laboratory extant, and the facilities incomparably superior to any other for rapid & cheap development of an invention, & working it up into Commercial shape with models patterns & special machinery — In fact there is no similar institution in Existence We do our own castings forgings Can build anything from a ladys watch to a locomotive . . ."

This laboratory was destined to be the inventor's headquarters for the remaining forty-four years of his life. During that period he was granted 520 additional patents, making a total of 1093 received over his lifetime. These covered, among other things, electric motors and generators, incandescent and fluorescent lamps, continuous nickel and copper plating, the depositing of metals in a vacuum, magnetic concentration and briquetting of iron ore, the motion picture camera and projector (the "movies" were actually born in West Orange), and cylinder and disc phonographs.

In 1928 Edison's contributions to the nation's welfare were recognized by a special Congressional Gold Medal. He was also the first civilian to receive the Navy's Distinguished Service Medal, granted for his service as Chairman of the Naval Consulting Board during World War I.

On October 18, 1931, while in the midst of an intensive research project to find a practical domestic source of natural rubber, Edison died at Glenmont at the age of eighty-four. His home and laboratory, donated by The Edison Company and his family to the United States Government, are now a National Historic Site administered by the National Park Service, and visited by thousands of people each year.

Within the Edison Archives at West Orange are many thousands of documents

Mina Edison in the conservatory at Glenmont.

Thomas Edison at Glenmont with Charles and Madeleine about 1893.

testifying to Thomas Edison's achievements as an inventor, scientist and businessman. Standing alone among these papers is this one Diary, a memoir which is almost completely unscientific. The eyes of youngsters frequently light up as they discover its open pages displayed in the inventor's library. From this Diary one realizes that a scientist has a lighter side to his personality and, like Edison's imaginary angels on the third page, can "lunch on the smell of flowers and new mown hay, drink the moisture of the air and dance to the hum of bees." Truly, as Edison added, "Nature is bound to smile somehow."

KATHLEEN L. MCGUIRK
Archivist, Edison National Historic Site

Mr. Thomas A. Edison
"Woodside Villa"
July 14 '85.

Mina Miller Edison.
(The Brook Foundation, Inc.)

Marginal figures beside certain lines in the Diary refer to explanatory Notes appearing on page 72.

Thomas A. Edison, in 1884.

Menlo Park N.J.

Sunday July 12 1885

Awakened at 5.15 AM. My eyes were embarassed by the sunbeams
- turned my back to them and tried to take another dip into oblivion
- succeeded — awakened at 7 AM. thought of Mina, Daisy, and
Mamma G— put all 3 in my mental kaledescope to obtain a
new combination a la Galton. took Mina as a basis, tried
to improve her beauty by discarding and adding certain
features borrowed from Daisy and Mamma G, a sort of
Raphaelized beauty, got into it too deep, mind flew away
and I went to sleep again.   Awakened at 8.15 AM.
Poweful itching of my head, lots of white dry dandruff—
what is this d—mnable material. Perhaps its the dust from
the dry literary matter I've crowded into my noddle lately
Its nomadic. gets all over my coat, must read about it in the
Encyclopedia.   Smoking too much makes me nervous —
must lasso my natural tendency to acquire such habits —
holding heavy cigar constantly in my mouth has deformed
my upper lip, it has a sort of Havanna curl.   Arose at
9 oclock came down stairs expecting twas too late for
breakfast — twas'nt. couldnt eat much, nerves of stomach
too nicotinny.   The roots of tobacco plants must go clear
through to hell.   Satans principal agent Dyspepsia

1

must have charge of this branch of the vegitable kingdom.
— It has just occured to me that the brain may digest
certain portions of food, say the etherial part, as well as the
stomach — perhaps dandruff is the excreta of the mind —
the quantity of this material being directly proportional to the
amount of reading one indulges in.   A book on German
metaphysics would thus easily ruin a dress suit.   After
breakfast start reading Hawthorne's English Note Book
dont think much of it — perhaps Im a literary barbarian
and am not eset educated up to the point of appreciating
fine writing— 90 per cent of his book is descriptive of old churches
and graveyards and coronors — He and Geo Selwyn ought
to have been appointed perpetual coroners of London.
Two fine things in the book were these.
Hawthorne shewing to little Rose Hawthorne a big live lobster   4
told her it was a very ugly thing and would bite everybody,
whereupon she asked   "if the first one God made bit him" —
again   "Ghostland is beyond the jurisdiction of veracity"
— I think freckles on the skin are due to some salt of Iron,
sunlight brings them out by reducing them from high to
low state of oxidation - perhaps with a powerful magnet
applied for some time, and then with proper chemicals, these
mud holes of beauty might be removed   Dot is   5

2

28

very is very busy cleaning the abode of our deaf and dumb parrot – she has fed it tons of edibles, and never got a sound out of it. This bird has the taciturnity of a statue, and the dirt producing capacity of a drove of buffalo.

This is by far the nicest day of this season, neither too hot or too cold.– it blooms on the apex of perfection – an Edenday Good day for an angels pic nic, They could lunch on the smell of flowers and new mown hay, drink the moisture of the air, and dance to the hum of bees, Fancy the Soul of Plato astride of a butterfly. riding around Menlo Park with a lunch basket   Nature is bound to smile somehow, Holzer has a little dog which just came on the veranda, The face of this dog was a dismal as a bust of Dante, but the dog wagged its tail continuously – This is evidently the way a dog laughs – I wonder if dogs ever go up to flowers and smell them – I think not – flowers were never intended for dogs and perhaps only incidentally for man, evidently Darwin has it right They make themselves pretty to attract the insect world who are the transportation agents of their pollen, pollen freight via Bee Line   There is a bumble bees nest somewhere near this veranda, several times one came near me – some little information (acquired experimentally) I obtained when a

6

small boy causes me to lose all delight in watching the navigation of this armed flower burglar.

Had dinner at 3 P.M. ruins of a chicken, rice pudding — I eat too quick — at 4 oclock Dot came around with her horse "Colonel" and took me out riding — beautiful roads — saw 10 acre lot full cultivated red raspberries. "A burying ground" so to speak. — got this execrable pun off on Dot   Dot says she is going to write a novel already started on — She has the judgement of a girl of 16 although only 12   We passed through the town of Metuchen, this town was named after an Indian chief, they called him Metuchen the chief of the rolling lands, the country being undulating.   Dot laughed heartily when I told her about a church being a heavenly fire-escape.   Returned from drive at 5 PM commenced read short sketches of life's Macauley Sidney Smith, Dickens & Charlotte Bronte,   Macauley when only 4 years ago omniverous reader, used book language in his childish conversation. when 5 years old, lady spilled some hot coffee on his legs, after awhile she asked him if he was better — he replied — "Madam the agony has abated" Macauleys mother must have built his mind several years before his body.   Sidney Smiths flashes of wit a perfect to call them chestnuts would be literary blasphemy.

They are wandering jewlets to wander forever in the printers' world — Dont like Dickens — dont know why — I'l stock my literary cellar with his works later. —

Charlotte Bronte was like DeQuincy. what a nice married couple they would have been I must read Jane Eyre.

— played a little on the piano — its badly out of tune — two Keys have lost their voice,

Dot just read to me outlines of her proposed novel, the basis seems to be a marriage under duress — I told her that in case of a marriage to put in bucketfulls of misery This would make it realistic, speaking of realism in painting etc Steele Mackaye at a dinner given to H H Porter, Wm Winter and myself told us of a difinition of modern realism given by some frenchman whose name I have forgotten,   " Realism, a dirty long haired painter sitting on the head of a bust of Shakespeare painting a pair of old 66¢ boots covered with dung "   The bell rings for supper Igve Sardines the principal attraction — on seeing them was attacked by a stroke of vivid memory of some sardines I eat last winter that caused a rebellion in the labyrinth of my stomach — could scarcely swallow them today

5

They nearly did the "return ball" act.   After supper
Dot pitched a ball to me several dozen times - first I ever
tried to catch, It was a hard as Nero's heart nearly broke
my baby-finger — gave it up — learned Dot and Maggie how
to play "Duck on the rock" They both thought it great fun,
and this is sunday —   My conscience seems to be oblivious
of sunday - it must be incrusted with a sort of irrelegious
tartar,   If I was not so deaf I might go to church
and get it taken off or at least loosened - eccavi I
will read the new version of the bible
Holzer is going to use the old laboratory for the purpose of
hatching chickens artificially by an electric incubator, He is
very enthusiastic — gave me full details — he is a very patient
and careful experimenter — think he will succeed - everything
succeeded in that old laboratory —   Just think
electricity employed to cheat a poor hen out of the pleasures
of maternity — Machine born chickens — What is home
without a mother   I suggested to H that he
vaccinate his hens with chicken pox virus, then the eggs
would have their embryo hereditarily innoculated + none
of the chickens would have the disease. for economys
sake he could start with one hen and rooster, He being

a scientific man with no farm experience I explained the necessity of having a rooster, he saw the force of this suggestion at once. The sun has left us on time, am going to read from the enclycopedia Brittanica to steady my nerves and go to bed early. I will shut my eyes and imagine a terraced abyss, each terrace occupied by a beautiful maiden to the first I will deliver my mind and they will pass it down down to the uttermost depths of silence and oblivion - Went to bed worked my imagination for a supply of maidens, only saw Mina Daisy & Mamma Scheme busted - sleep.

Woodside Villa
    Boston Harbor

Menlo Park NJ July 13 1885

Woke (is there such a word) at 6 oclock — slipped down the declivity of unconcienceness again until 7. arose and tried to shave with a razor so dull, that every time I scraped my face it looked as if I was in the throes of cholera morbus. By shaving often I too a certain extent circumvent the diabolical malignity of these razors — If I could get my mind down to details perhaps could learn to sharpen it, but on the otherhand I might cut myself — As I had to catch the 7.30 am train for New York I hurried breakfast, crowded meat potatoes, eggs, Coffee, tandem down into the chemical room of my body Ive now got dyspepsia in that diabolical thing that Carlyle calls the stomach, rushed and caught train — Bought a New York World at Elizabeth for my mental breakfast — Among the million of perfected Mortals on Manhattan island two of them took it into their heads to cut their naval chord from mother earth and be born into a new world, while two other less developed citizens stopped two of the neighbors from living — The details of these two little

incidents conveyed to my mind what beautiful
creatures we ~~know~~ live among, and how with the aid
of the police, civilization so rapidly advances —
Went to New York via DesGrosses Street ferry took
cars across town — saw a women get into car that
was so tall and frightfully thin as well as dried up
that my mechanical mind at once conceived the idea
that it would be the proper thing to run a lancet
into her arm and knew joints and insert automatic
self feeding oil cups to diminish the creaking when
she walked — Got off at Broadway — tried experiment
of walking two miles to our office 65 5th ave with
idea it would alleviate my dyspeptic pains — It didnt
Went into Scribner & Sons on way up saw about a
thousand books I wanted right off   Mind No 1 said
why not buy a box full and send to Boston now — Mind
No 2 (acquired and worldly mind) gave a most withering
mental glance at mind No 1 and said you fool, buy
only two books, these you can carry without trouble
and will last until you get to Boston, Buying books
in NYork to send to Boston is like "carrying coals to
Newcastle" of course I took the advice of this

8

9

35

Earthy adviser — Bought Aldrich's Story of a bad boy which is a spongecake kind of literature, very witty and charming — and a work on Goethe & Schiller by Boynsen which is soggy literature a little wit & anecdote in this style of literature would have the same effect as baking soda on bread, give pleasing results. —

Waited one hour for the appearance of a lawyer who is to cross-examine me on events that occurred 11 years ago — went on stand at 1130 — He handed me a piece of paper with some figures on it, not another mark, asked in a childlike voice if these were my figures, what they were about and what day 11 years ago I made them — This implied compliment to the splendor of my memory was at first so pleasing to my vanity that I tried every means to trap my memory into stating just what he wanted — but then I thought what good is a compliment from a 10 cent lawyer, and I waived back my recollection. A lawsuit is the suicide of Time, — got through at 330 PM — waded through a lot of accumulated correspondence mostly relating to other peoples business — Insull saw Wiman about getting car

9, 10

for Railroad Telegh experiment — will get costs in day
or so. — Tomlinson made Sammy mad by saying
he Insull was Valet to my intellect — got $100
met Dot and skipped for the Argosy of the
Puritan Sea, (ie) Sound Steamboat — Dot is reading
a novel — rather trashy, Love hash. — I completed
reading Aldrich's Bad Boy and advanced 50 pages
in Goethe then retired to a "Sound" Sleep

Woodside Villa July 14 1885.

Dot introduced me to a new day at 5.30 am.
Arose – toileted quickly – breakfasted – then went from
boat to street car – asked colored gentleman, how
long before car left – worked his articulating
apparatus so weakly I didn't hear word he said,
– its nice to be a little deaf when travelling
you can ask everbody directions then pump
your imagination for the answer, it strengthens
this faculty. — Took train leaving at 7 from
Providence for the metropolis of culture – arrived
there 9 am "Coupaid" it to Damons office
– waited 3/4 hour for his arrival, Then left for the
Château-sur-le-Mer — If I stay there much
longer Mrs G— will think me a bore – perhaps
she thinks I make only two visits each year in
one place each of 6 months – Noticed there
was no stewardess on the ferry boat, strange
omission considering the length of the voyage
and the swell made by the tri-monthly boat to
Nantasket. — Man with a dusty railroad Co
Expression let down a sort of portcullis

12

and the passengers poured themselves out — arrived
Winthrop junction found Patrick there according to
telephonic instructions, another evidence that the
telephone works sometimes, Patrick had the Americanized
Dog cart and incidentally a horse, suppose patrick
would forget the horse, because last week he went
into Boston to Damons city residence and turned
on the gas & started up the meter from a state
of innocence to the wildest prevarication, + forgot to turn gas off — arrived
at Woodside Villa and was greeted by Mamma
with a smile as sweet as a cherub that buzzed
around the bedside of Raphael — A fresh
invoice of innocence and beauty had arrived in
my absence in the persons of Miss Louise Igoe and
her aunt Miss Igoe like Miss Daisy is from
Indianapolis, that producer of hoosier venus's
Miss Igoe is a pronounced blonde, blue eyes, with
a complexion as clear as the conscience of a
baby angel, with hair like Andromache
Miss Igoes aunt is a bright elderly lady who
beat me so bad at checkers that my bump of
"Stragetic combination" has sunk in about two

13

inches — for fear that Mrs G— might think I had
an inexhaustable supply of dirty shirts, I put on one
of those starched horrors procured for me by Tomlinson
— put my spongy mind at work on life Goethe —
Chewed some Tutu gum presented me by Mrs G—
Conceived the idea that the mastication of this chunk
of illimitable plasticity — a dentiferous tread-mill
so to speak, would act on the salivial glands to
produce an excess of this neccessary ingredient
of the digestive fluid and thus a selfacting home
made remedy for dyspepsia would be obtained
— believe there is something in this as my dyspeptic
pains are receeding from ~~from~~ recogniction
— Dot is learning to play Lange's "Blumenlied"
on the piano — Miss Igoe I learn from a
desultory conversation is involved in a correspondence
with a brother of Miss Mina who resides at Canton
Ohio being connected with the Mower & reaper
firm of Aultman & Miller The letter received today
being about as long as the bills at the Grand
Hotel at Paris are I surmise of rather a
serious character, cupidly speaking

15

16

The frequency of their reception will confirm or disaffirm my conjectures as to the proximity of a serious catastrophe —— A postoffice courtship is a novelty to me, so I have resolved to follow up this matter for the experience which I will obtain — This may come handy should "My head ever become the dupe of my heart" as papa Rochefacauld puts it. —— In evening went out on sea wall — noticed a strange phosphorecent light in the west, probably caused by a baby moon just going down Chinaward thought at first the Aurora Borealis had moved out west — went to bed early dreamed of a ~~dreadful~~ Demon with eyes four hundred feet apart.

15

Woodside Villa July 15 1885

Slept well — Breakfasted clear up to my adams
apple — took shawl strap and went to Boston
with Damon with following memorandum of things
to get.

Lavatar on the human face — Miss Clevelands
book — Heloise by Rosseau — short neckties — Wilhelm
Meister — Basket fruit — Sorrows of Werther —
Madam Recamiers works — Diary books — pencils
Telephone documents   Mark Twains gummed
Potentiality of Literature (ie) scrap book. — also book
called "How success is won" containing life of Dr
Vincent & something in about Minas father and your
humble servitor.   Found that only copy of
Lavatar which I saw the other day had been
sold to some one who was on the same lay as
myself Bought Disreali's Curriosities of
Literature instead — Got Miss C' book — Twains
scrap book — Diary books, How Success is won
also fruit among which are some peaches which
the vendor said came from California — think

of a pie 3000 miles long—There seemed to be a
South Carolina accent in their taste— Started
back to office with fruit, apparantly by the same
route I came, brought up in a strange street
saw landmark and got on right course again
Boston ought to be buoyed and charts furnished
strangers — Damon suggests American District
Messenger buoys with uniform — Saw a lady
who looked like Mina—got thinking about Mina
and came near being run over by a street car
— If Mina interferes much more will have to take
out an accident policy — Went to dinner at a
sort of No-bread-with-one-fishball restaurant
then came up towards Damons office, met Damon
Madden and Ex Gov Howard of Rhode Island,
The Governor whom I know and who is very deaf
greeted me with a boiler yard voice, He has to
raise his voice so he can hear himself to enable
him to check off the acuracy of his pronounciation
The Governor never has much time, always in a hurry
—full of business, inebriated with industry—If he
should be on his death bed I beluie he would

17

call in a short hand clerk to dictate directions for
his funeral, short sketch of his life, taking a press
copy of the same in case of litigation
Madden looks well in the face but I am told its
an Undertakers blush — Went to Damons office
he was telling me about a man who had a genius
for stupidity when Vail came in dressed like
Beau Brummel, both went into another room
to try some experiments on Damons Phonometer
— Saw Hovey a very very bright newspaper man
told me a story related to him by a man who I
never would have imagined could or would have
told such stories   I refer to a gentleman in the
employment of the Telephone Co who Tomlinson
nicknamed "Prepositum" because he got off that word
in a business conversation, his eminent respectability
so impressed Tomlinson that when he came out
of his office asked me to take him quickly somewhere
disreputable so he could recover.   This story
would have embarassed Satan — I shall not relate it.
but I have called it "Prepositums Turkish Compromise"
Hovey told me a lot about a 6th sense, mind reading etc

made some suggestions about Railroad Telegraph — Came home with Damon at 5 o'clock — Damon has an ulcerated molar — Just before supper Mrs Roberts and another lady came in to visit Mrs G. Mrs R is a charming woman — Condensed ~~sun~~ sunshine — beautiful — plays piano like a long haired professor — played several of Lange's pieces first time seeing them, This seems as incomprehensible to me as a man reciting the Lords prayer in four languages simultaneously — Mrs R promised, to come tomorrow evening and bring with her a lady who sings beautifully and a boy dripping with music — Everyone after supper started their Diary Mrs G Igoe — Daisy & Dot went to bed at 1130. forgot two nights running to ask Damon for night shirt — That part of my memory which has charge of the night shirt department is evidently out of order.

19

Woodside Villa July 16 1885

I find on waking up this morning that I went to bed last night with the curtains up in my room— Glad the family next door retire early — I blushed retroactively to think of it— Slept well— weather clear - warm. Thermometer prolongatively progressive — day so fine that barometer anaethized — breakfasted —. Diaried a lot of nonsense — Read some of Longfellows Hyperon, read to where he tells about a statue of a saint that was attacked with somnambulism and went around nights with a lantern repairing roofs, especially that of a widow woman who neglected her family to pray all day in the church   Read account of two murders in Morning Herald to keep up my interest in human affairs — Built an air castle or two— Took my new shoes out on a trial trip — Read some of Miss Clevelands book where she goes for George Eliot for not having a heavenly streak of imaginative Twaddle in her poetry—   The girls assisted by myself trimmed the Elizabeth collars on twelve dasies, inked eyes nose & mouth on the yellow part which gave them a quaint human look, paper dresses were put on them and all were mounted on the side of a paper box and labelled "The Twelve Daughters of Venus" I hope no College bred dude will come down here and throw out insinuations that Venus was never married, and never had any children anyway — Girls went in bathing. Me and Damon went out in the steam Yacht sailed around over the lobster nursery for an hour or so — In the evening Damon started a diary — very witty — Miss Igoe told Damon she couldnt express her admiration, whereupon he told her to send it by ~~express~~ freight. Lunched our souls on a Strauss waltz played by Miss Daisy, then we all set around the table to write up our diaries, I learned the girls how to make shadow pictures by use of crumpled paper = we tried some experiments in mind reading which were not very successful, Think mind reading contrary to common sense, wise provision of the Bon Dieu that we cannot read each others minds Twould stop civilization and everybody would take to the Woods = in fifty or hundred thousand centuries when mankind have become perfect by evolution then perhaps this sense could be developed with safety to the state, Damon

21

and I went into a minute expense account of our proposed
earthly paradise in the land of Flowers, also a duplicate north
and we concluded to take short views of life and go ahead
with the scheme,   It will make a savage onslaught on our
bank account. Damon remarked that now all the wind
work is done there only remains some little details to
attend to such a "raising the money" etc, Mrs Roberts hurt
her Sophrano arm and could not come over an play for us
as promised and thus we lost her perfumed conversation
lovely music and serephic smile — La femme qui-rit —
Since Miss Igoe has been reading Miss Clevelands book
her language has become ~~disyllabic and~~ dissyllabic ponderous, stiff and
formal, each observation seems laundried —
If this weather gets much hotter, Hell will get
up a reputation as a ~~cool~~ summer resort, Dot asked
how books went in the mail, Damon said as second class
~~mail~~ mail matter, I said Me and Damon would go
at this rating — suggested that Mina would have to
pay full postage, Damon thought she should be
registered — This reminds me that I read the other
day of a man who applied for a situation as
sexton in the Dead letter office, — Daisies sisters

19

photograph rests on the mantel, shews very beautiful
girl every fly that has attempted to light on it
has slipped and fallen, going to put piece chalk near
it so they can chalk their feet, this will permit with
safety the insectivorous branch of nature to gaze upon
a picture of what they will attained after ages of
evolution. Ladies went to bed, this removed the
articutating upholstery, then we went to bed,

Woodside Villa July 17 1885

Slept so sound that even Mina didn't bother me as. It would stagger the mind of Raphael in a dream to imagine a being comparable to the Maid of Chataqua so I must have slept very sound — As usual I was the last one up, This is because I'm so deaf — found everbody smiling and happy — Read more of Miss Clevelands book, think she is a smart woman — relatively — Damons diary progressing finely — Patricks went to city get tickets for Opera of Polly, we can Comparrot with Sullivans = We are going out with the ladies in yachts to sail perchance to fish,   The lines will be bated at both ends. Constantly talking about Mina who me an Damon use as a sort of yardstick for measuring perfection makes Dot jealous, She threatens to become an incipient Lucretia Borgia,   Hottest day of season — never Hell must have sprung a leak, at two oclock went out on yacht — cooler on the water, Sailed out to the Rock-buoy . This is the point where Damon goes to change his mind, he circles

the boat around several times, like a carrier pigeon
before starting out on a journey, then we start right
dropped anchor in a shady part of the open bay
— I acted as Master of the fish lines, delivered them
bated to all. The clam boquets were thrown to
the picatorial actors — Miss Daisy caught the first
he came up smilingly to seize the boquet when she
jerked him into the dress circle, genus unknown -
I caught the next - genus uncertain, The next was
not caught.   Fish seem to be rather conservative
around this bay, one seldom catches enough to
form the fundamental basis for a pie — Dante left
out one of the torments of hades - I could imagine
a doomed mortal made to untangle wet fish lines
forever — Everybody lost patience at the stupidity
of the fish in not coming forward promptly to be
murdered - We hauled up anchor, and Damon
steering by the compass, (he being by it) made for
the vicinity of Apple island - While approaching
it we saw a race between two little model vessels
full rigged and about 2 feet long - Two yawl boats
filled apparantly with US naval officers and men

were following them, Are these effeminate pursuits a precursor of the decline and fall of a country as history tells us. — Landed at dock 4 30. Came into Villa and commenced reading Lavatar on Facial Philosophy — Dot saw a jelly fish and vehemently called our attention to this translucent chestnut, — Barge called to take us to theatre via Winthrop Junction and Railroad. when we arrived at junction found we should have to wait some time, so we took an Open street car for city — While passing along saw man on Bicycle, asked Damon if he Ever rode one — He said he did, once practiced riding in large freight shed where floor was even with door of cars and three feet from ground, one day from reason he never could explain he went right through one of the doors to the ground, I remarked that I supposed he kept right on riding No said Damon I jumped back?   Arriving at Ferry boat I asked Damon if it was further across River high at tide said he thought it was a he noticed the piles in the ship were at a slight angle — Arriving on the other side took Street Gondola, arrived near top of Hanover Street when horses were unable to pull cars to the

26

Woodside Villa July 18 1883

top of the hill, car slipped back, The executive department
of my body was about to issue a writ of ejectment
when some of the passengers jumped out and stopped
Car, one passenger halloed out to let her go they
would get more ride — Arriving a little too early
for theatre, went to an Ice cream bazar frigidified
ourselves, Then went to Theatre, where we found it
very hot, Solomon the Composer came from the cellar
of fairies and sprung a chestnut overture on the
few mortals in the audience chamber, Then the
Curtain arose shewing the usual number of servant
girls in tights — The raising of the panapoly
of fairyland let some more heat in — a rushing
sound was heard and Damon said they were turning
on the steam — The fairies mopped their foreheads —
perspiration dripped down on stage from the painted
Cherubs over the arch — after numerous military
evolutions by the chorus Miss Lillian Russell made
her appearance — Beautiful woman, sweet voice,
Wore a fur lined cloak which I thought about as
appropriate in this weather as to clothe the

firemen on the Red Sea Steamers in sealskin
overcoats – noticed one or two original strains
the balance of the music seemed to be Bagpipean
Improvastorationes – Didn't hear anything that
was spoken except once when I thought I heard
one of the actors say that his mother sung
sung in the Chineese ballef – Our seats
were in the baldhead section, After theatre
walked to ferry boat – Saw a steamer passing
brilliantly lighted Mrs G asked what could be
nicer that a lighted steamer on the waters at
night – sombody suggested two steamers –
arrived at sister ferry, took RR train, Saw Miss
Russell with her last husband Mr Solomon get on
train, they stop I believe at the sea shore near us
– Home – Bed – Sleep –

Woodside July 18 1885

Last night room was very close, single sheet over me
seemed inch thick— Bug proof windows seems to repel
obtrusiveness on the part of any prowling Zephyr that
might want to come in and lunch on perspiration,
Rolled like a ship in a Typhoon, if this weather keeps
on I'll wear holes in the bed clothes, Arose early
Weather blasphemingly hot— went out in sun, came
back dripping with water, tried to get into the umbrella
rack to drain off, took off two courses of clothes
This would be good day to adopt Sidney Smiths plan
of taking off your flesh and sitting down in your bones.
Mem— go to a print cloth mill and have yourself
run through the Calico printing machine, This would
be the Ultama Thule of thin clothing, Read some in
Lavatar, Mme Recamier, Rosseaus Emile, Laid down
on sofa-fell asleep—Dreamed that Damon had the
sunstroke and was laid on the floor of his office.
where he swelled up so that he broke the floor
above and two Editors of a baseball journal fell
through and were killed, Thought the chief of the

fire department came in and ordered holes to be bored in him Then something changed the dream saw a lot of animals which such marvellous characteristics as would be sufficient to bust up the whole science of paleontology — Cuvier, Buffon & Darwin never could have started their theories had a few samples of these animals ever browsed around on this little mud ball of ours — After a survey of this vast imaginative Menagerie I woke up by nearly falling off the sofa, found the heat had reached the apex of its malignity — Went out yachting — all the ladies in attendance — I was delightfully unhot, Ladies played game called memory — Scheme №1 calls out name of prominent author № 2 Repeats this name and adds another & so on. soon one has to remember a dozen names all of which must be repeated in the order given — result Miss Daisy had the best & I the poorest memory —— We played another game called "pon honor", resultant of which is that if you are caught you must truthfully answer a question put by each player, These questions generally relate to the amours of the players — Arrived home at 7.30

Yacht brought in too far and left stranded by the receeding of the tide, Suppered, went out and saw saw some fvie works set off by an unknown sojourner in these Ozonic parts, afterwards went over to Cottage Park at the kind invitation of the Charming Mrs Roberts to hear the band play pro bono publico and her boy exclusivemento, Boy is quite a progedy on the piano, plays with great rapidity, his hand and fingers went like a buz saw, played a solemn piece which I imagined might be God kill the Queen, In walking back Miss Igoe got several boulders in her shoes, Miss Daisy Smiled so sweetly all the evening that I imagined a ray of ol sunshine tried to pass her and got stuck, Mrs Roberts caught cold in her arm its cough is better, home-bed-oblivion-

~~Woodchurch Surrey~~ Woodside Villa July 19th 1885

Slept as sound as a bug in a barrell of morphine, Donned a boiled and starched emblem of respectability = Eat food for breakfast, Weather delightful — Canary seed orchestra started up with same old tune, ancestors of this bird sang the self same tune 6000 years ago to Adam down on the Euphrates, way back when Abel got a situation as the first angel — Read Sunday Herald, learned of John Roach's failure — am sorry — he has been pursued with great malignity by newspapers and others, from ignorance I think — Americans ought to be proud of Roach who started in life as a day laborer and become the giant of industry and the greatest shipbuilder in the United States employing thousands of men and feeding innumerable families — What has he now for this 40 years of incessant work and worry People who hound such men as these I would invent a special Hades, I would stricken them with the chronic sciatic neuralgia and cause them to wander forever stark naked within the artic circle' — Saw in same paper account of base ball match, this struck me as something unusual —— Read more about that immeasureable immensity of tact and beauty madame

58

Recamier, I would like to see such a woman = Nature
seems to be running her factory on another style of goods
nowdays and wont switch back until long after I'm
baldheaded — Damon went out to assist the tide in —
Daisy told me something about a man who kept
livery stable in Venice,   In afternoon went out in
yacht, on first trip all our folks, and lot of smaller
people sailed around for an hour returned and landed
the abreviated people - Started for Cottage Park where
we took on board the Charming Mrs Roberts brevet
Recamier, and a large lady friend whose name has
twice got up and jumped out of my mind, Then sailed
away for Rock buoy and for some ocult reason Damon
didnt stop and change his mind but headed for Liverpool
went out two miles in ocean, undulations threatened
to disturb the stability of the dinner of divers persons,
returned at 7 p.m. Then Damon took out a boat load
of Slaves of the Kitchin — Damon and I after his
return study plans for our Floridian bower in the
lowlands of the peninsular Eden, within that charmed zone
of beauty, where wafted from the table lands of the Oronoco
and the dark Carib sea, perfumed zephyrs forever

33

Kiss the gorgeous flora, Rats! — Damon took the plans to Boston to place them into the hands of an architectualist to be reduced to a paper reality — Damon promised to ascertain probable cost chartering schooner to plough the spanish main loaded with our hen coops — Dot came in and gave us a lot of girlish philosophy which amused us greatly — Oh dear this celestial mud ball has made another revolution and no photograph yet received from the Chataquain Parragon of Perfection, How much longer will Hope dance on my intellect   Miss Igoe told me of a picture she had taken on a rock at Panama ny. There were several others in the group, interpolated so as to dilute the effect of Mina's beauty, as she stated the picture was taken on a rock I immediately brought my scientific imagination to work to ascertain how the artist could have flowed collodion over a rock and put so many people inside his camera, Miss Igoe kindly corrected her explanation by stating that a picture was taken by a camera of a group on a rock, thus my mind was brought back from a suspicion of her verbal integrity to a belief in the honesty of her narrative

34

After supper Mrs H, Daisy and Louise with myself
as an incidental appendage walked over to the town
of Ocean Spray, went into a drug store and
bought some alleged candy, asked the gilded youth
with the usual vacuous expression, if he had any
nitric peroxide, he gave a wild stare of incomphrensibility
Then I simplified the name to nitric acid, which I
hoped was within the scope of his understanding
a faint gleam of intelligence crept over his face
whereupon he went into another room from which he
returned with the remark that he didnt keep nitric
acid — Fancy a drug store without nitric acid,
A drug store nowdays seems to consist of a
frontage of Red blue and green demijohns a soda
fountain, Case with candy and toothbrushes, a lot
of almost empty bottles with death and stomachatic destruction
written in latin on them, all in charge of a young man
with a hatchet shaped head, hair parted laid out by
a civil engineer, and a blank stare of mediocrity
on his face, that by comparison would cause a gum
indian in the Eden Musée look intellectual — On our
return I carried the terrealbian gum drops — moon was

shining brightly — girls called my attention several
times to beauty of the light from said moon shining
upon the waters, couldn't appreciate it, was so busy
taking a mental triangleation of the moon the two
sides of said triangle meeting the base line of the
Earth at Woodside and Akron Ohio, Miss Igoe
told us about her love of ancient literature, how
she loved to read Latin but couldn't, I told her I
was so fond of Greek that I always rushed for the
comedies of Aristophanes to read whenever I had
the jumping toothache; Bed — Mina, Morning,

36

Woodside July 20 1885

Arose before anybody else — came down and went out
to look at Mamma Earth and her green clothes —
Breakfasted — Read aloud from Madame Recamiers
memoirs for the ladies — Kept this up for an hour
got as hoarse as a fog horn, Think the ladies
got jealous of Madame Recamier — its so hot — I put
everything off — Hot weather is the mother of
procrastination — my energy is at ebb tide — I'm
getting caloricly stupid — Tried to read some of the
involved sentences in Miss Clevelands book, mind
stumbled on a ponderous perioration and fell in
between two paragraphs and lay unconcious
for ten minutes — Smoked a cigar under the
alias of 'Reina Victoria' think it must have been
seasoned in a sewer — Mrs Clark told me
a story about Louise's mother singing in a company
a song called 'I have no home, I have no home,'
somebody halloed out that he would provide her with a
good home if she would stop. I understood Mrs
Clark to say that this gentleman was a

bookkeeper in a small pox hospital — Mrs G has placed fly paper all over the house, These cunning Engines of insectiverous destruction are doing a big business — One of the first things I do when I reach heaven is to ascertain what flies are made for — this done I'll be ready for business, perhaps I am too sanguine and may bring up at the other terminal and one of my punishments will be a general ukase from Satan to keep mum when Edison tries to get any entomological information — Satan is the scarecrow in the religious cornfield — Towards sundown went with the ladies on yacht — Talked about love, cupid, appollo, Adonis, ideal persons One of the ladies said she had never come across her ideal — I suggested she wait until the second Advent, — Damon steared the galleon, Damon's heart is so big it inclines him to embonpoint — On shore it was hot enough to test Safes but on the water twas cool as a cucumber in an artic cache — Mrs G has promised for three consecutive days to have some clams a la Taft She has perspired her memory all away —

Been hunting around for some ants nests, so
I can have a good watch of them laying on the
grass — Dont seem to be any around — dont think
an ant could make a decent living in a land
where a yankee has to emigrate from to survive, —
For the first time in my life I have bought a pair of
premeditalely tight shoes — These shoes are small
and look nice my N° 2 mind (acquired mind)
has succeeded in convincing my N° 1 mind, (primal
mind or heart) that it is pure vanity, conceit and
folly to suffer bodily pains that ones person may
have graces the outcome of secret agony — Read the
funny column in the Traveller and went to bed,

Woodside July 21 1885

Slept splendidly — evidently I was innoculated with isomnie bactilli when a baby — arose early went out to flirt with the flowers, & I wonder if there are not microscopic orchids growing on the motes of the air — Saw big field of squashes throwing out their leafy tenticles to the wind preparing to catch the little fleeting atom for assimulation into its progeny the squash gourd — A spider weaves its net to catch an organized whole, how like this is the vegitable living plant, the leaves and stalk catch the primal free atom, all are then arranged in an organized whole,   Heard a call from the house that sounded like the shreick of a lost angel, it was a female voice three sizes too small for the distance and was a call for breakfast — after breakfast laid down on sofa, fell into light draught sleep dreamed that in the depth of space, on a bleak and gigantic planet the solitary soul of the great Napoleon was the sole inhabitant, I saw him as in the pictures, in

40

contemplative aspect with his blue eagle eye, amid the howl of the tempest and the lashing of gigantic waves high up on a jutting promontory gazing out among the worlds & stars that stud the depths of infinity Miles above him circled and swept the sky with ponderous wing the imperial condor bearing in his talons a message, then the scene busted — This comes from reading about Napoleon in Madame Recamiers memoirs, Then my dream changed - Thought I was looking out upon the sea, suddenly the air was filled with millions of little cherubs as one sees in Raphaels pictures each I thought was about the size of a fly. They were perfectly formed & seemed semi-transparent, each swept down to the surface of the sea, reached out both their tiny hands and grabbed a very small drop of water, and flew upwards where they assembled and appeared to form a cloud, This method of forming clouds was so different from the method described in Ganots Physics that I congratulated myself on having learned the ~~truth~~ true method and was thinking how I would gloat over the chagrin of those cold blooded Savans who would desect an angel or boil a live baby to study the perturbations of the human larynx. Then this scheme was wrecked by my awakening — The weather being cool went out on Veranda to exercise my appreciation of Nature, Saw bugs, butterflies as varied as Prangs Chromos, Birds innumerable, flowers with as great a variety of color as Calico for the African market, then to spoil the whole two poor miserable mortals came, who probably carry the idea that this world was created for them exclusively and that a large portion of the Creators time was specially devoted to hearing requests, criticisms and complaints about the imperfection of the natural laws which regulate this mud ball — What a wonderfully small idea mankind has of the Almighty— My impression is that he has made unchangeable laws to govern this and billions of other worlds and that he has forgotten even the ~~exh~~ existence of this little mote of ours ages ago. Why cant man follow up and practice the teachings of his own conscience, mind his business, and not obtrude his purposely created finite mind in affairs that will be attended to without any volunteed advice, — Came into the house at the request of the ladies and read aloud for two hours from the Memoirs Recamier — then talked on the subject of the tender passion, the ladies never seem to tire of this subject — then supper ~~some~~ ~~Some~~ Trovatores du Pave made their appearance and commenced to play — I requested the distinguished honor of their presence on the Veranda — After supper weather being cool but rather windy, took our trovatores on the yacht and all hands sailed out on the bay — Had to go around an arm of the bay to get coal — water splashed so I got _dashed_ _wet_. Three several times the water brake loose from the iron grasp of gravitation and jumped on my 65 dollar coat But when one of the ladies got a small fragment of a drop on her dress ~~of course~~ orders were issued to make for port — landed and

took our Troubadors to house several ladies
hiring houses for the summer brought their
husbands with them and helped sop up the
music — afterwards Mrs & Mr G hospitablized
by firing off several champaign bottles and
some of those delightful Cookies, I do believe
I have a "big bump for Cookies, the first entry
made by the recording angel on my behalf
was for stealing my mothers cookies, 11 oclock
came and the pattering of many footsteps upon
the stairs signalled the coming birth of silence
only to be disturbed by the sonorous snore
of the aimable Damon and the demonic
laughter of the amatory family Cat ———

Thomas and Mina Edison.

The original Diary of Thomas A. Edison now at the Edison National Historic Site, West Orange, New Jersey.

NOTES

1. Mina: Mina Miller, daughter of Lewis Miller of Akron, Ohio, who was to become Edison's second wife in February, 1886.
2. Daisy: Daisy Gaston, a young friend of Mrs. Gilliland's from Indianapolis.
3. Mama G: Wife of Ezra T. Gilliland; formerly Miss Lillian Johnson of Indianapolis.
4. Rose Hawthorne: Daughter of Nathaniel Hawthorne. She later married George Parsons Lathrop, a writer and reporter who prepared a biographical study of Edison for *Harper's Magazine* in 1890.
5. Dot: Edison's nickname for his eldest daughter, Marion Estelle, who was twelve-years-old at this time.
6. Holzer: William Holzer, a glass blower at the Edison Lamp Factory who was married to Edison's first wife's sister, Alice Stilwell Holzer.
7. Woodside Villa, Boston Harbor: The Gilliland's rented cottage at number 3 Woodside, Winthrop, Mass. The notation at this point in the Diary indicates Edison may have been writing at Woodside rather than at Menlo Park.
8. 65 5th Ave.: Offices of the Edison Light Company in New York City.
9. Insull: Samuel Insull, then Edison's personal secretary and business manager.
10. Wiman: Erastus Wiman, then President of the Northwestern Telegraph Company of Canada.
11. Tomlinson: John C. Tomlinson, Edison's attorney.
12. Damon: Edison's nickname for Ezra T. Gilliland. The office was that of the American Bell Telephone Company, 45 Milk Street, Boston.
13. Patrick: An employee of Ezra Gilliland.
14. Miss Louise Igoe: A friend of the Gillilands who later married Robert Anderson Miller, brother of Mina Miller.
15. . . . brother of Miss Mina: Robert Anderson Miller.
16. Aultman and Miller: Lewis Miller's firm in Canton, Ohio.
17. Dr. Vincent: Bishop John Vincent, co-founder with Lewis Miller of the Chatauqua Association.
18. Vail: Theodore Vail, manager of the Bell Telephone Company in Boston.
19. . . . paradise in the land of Flowers: Fort Meyers, Florida where Edison and Gilliland built summer homes and a laboratory.
20. Cottage Park: Famous hotel and resort which was destroyed by fire in the 1920's.